Midlife musings

Cherry Walker

Presentation by *BookLeaf Publishing*

Web: www.bookleafpub.com

E-mail: info@bookleafpub.com

ISBN: 9789357615969

First edition 2022

Tea making tools

Tissue textured, with rings that spin,
Lines that tell tales of losses and wins,
Hands that have farmed, cooked, cleaned and
mothered,
Baking biscuits and cakes with butter cream
smothered,
These are the hands that stroked my ears and
gently spoke of all the years,
The fun, the dancing, the resilience and joy,
So preciously decorated with jewels,
These wonderful tea making tools.

The beating machine

The heart

How vulnerable and shaky is this piece of me that keeps a timely, safe and steady rhythm to life until it comes to love.

Love, the dangerous part of the heart.

I feel and know love divinely and without measure or boundaries or rules for my children, family and friends; all of these people are reliable in keeping this beating machine safe.

But love...the blow you away love, the fast pace love, the excitement of love has become nothing more than a dangerous game. That door of that compartment of my heart is firmly shut, the risk of disappointment and heart break and ache is too high.

I believed in every romantic novel I read, the poems that that were romantically enthralling, Shakespeare and his sonnets, picnics, road trips, sunsets and never-ending dates.

Maybe one day the door will creak open, lubricated by loves version of WD40. Until that time my heart is for my children, the best love affair and love story that will last the length of time.

My sunshine

Some days felt cloudy, some days felt better, some felt like storms; a belter with nowhere to shelter.

No arms to hold her to remind her of her strength when days had been rocky and tedious in length.

She loves her girls with all her might, moving mountains, working hard, a romance was not in sight.

Time was not on this woman's side, so she built her world around her loves and was gifted with family and friends who just fitted and felt like the snuggest of gloves.

She built some walls, robust and strong, having no idea her sunshine would suddenly come along.

Her mum, who was wise and sage and quite annoyingly never wrong, spoke of a man who's world would be singing the very same song. A

tune of love for his girl, where a possible love
and romance would unfurl.

And then she met this wonderous man, full of
sunshine, fun, quirks and kindness. He filled her
with awe and a nervous shyness.

The physical attraction was there from the start,
She thought She did smilng well, but he made it
a fine art.

His eyes full of joy as he spoke to Cherry, his
arms telling stories so wild and free.

His beautiful voice made him a delectable
choice as she sat and listened, she felt his
warmth, tones of sunshine glistened.

But then came the greatest appeal, the love for
his daughter Lia was concrete real. He spoke of
her with such joy and pride of all the times she's
by his side.

And after that came a trip to Staithes, where she
felt love for him in abundance, like crashing
waves. A friendship, soulmate she'd so often
craved. In complete joy, freedom and happiness
they bathed.

And now we're pretty much up to date, her sunshine came not too soon or late. The perfect timing for two souls to meet, in front of them a world of wonder to greet.

No Spanx Romance

t's the summer of 2022,

Who knew that it would be the start of new non Spanx romance?

Heatwave baby, we're all hot and sweaty and I can't be a bonded Betty,

I need to breathe, let the tummy out, let the bum slip down and wear these curves like a crown.

Wrinkled, loose, jelly like putty for an experienced masseuse,

It's the summer of 2022

Who knew it would be the start of no Spanx romance?

Don't pity her

Don't pity her, admire her

She has nerves of steel and a heart that's real.
She's bold and brave and has no desire to be
saved.
She's whole and bold and has a story to be told.

Don't pity her, admire her.

For this woman does it all,
Mothering was her natures call,
The more she does the stronger she grows,
This enables her to manage the lows.

Don't pity her, admire her.

And if you have a judgy soul, maybe it's because
you wish to be this whole?

The Riley's

Do you know a Riley?

In the life of Riley club?

You know the type of parent that choices
adulthood over parenthood.

Watch out, this seems to be an ever growing
club, the type where they'd rather take their
girlfriend to the pub.

The Riley is an unusual breed, often spineless
with the girlfriend in the lead.

The Riley will let you do all the work, raise their
children and have a regular break. These men
are selfish, make no mistake.

The Riley will pay you a measly sum and then
turn up every two weeks and play parenting
dumb.

They'll let you do all the work, and I mean it all,
whilst they go and have a ball.

The Riley; selfish, spineless, priorities wrong,
could do better but continues to sing the same
old song.

The life of Riley.

The winner takes all the glory

I'm grey, I'm frazzled, my body is wobbly, I'm busy, I'm stressed, I'm mothering, I'm tired, I'm working, I'm overwhelmed.

I am happy. I am woman.

The winner takes all the glory.

The Mothers in my life

To be a good mum, you have to know good mums and I'm proud to say I do.

The wise mums, the sage mums, the dancing on the worktop mums, the bold mums, the strong mums, the always feeling like they're getting it wrong mums, the mums who smother, the mums who cheer, the mums who survive it, the mums I hold near.

But the most important mum type of all, the mum who lets you show up exactly as you, warts and all, she makes you a brew and she reminds you, you are a great mum too.

Teeth

It was the October of 2022

I've not seen your teeth, your teeth so much,
Not so much your teeth, but this radiant smile, it
pushes your chubby cheeks up to your eyes, you
glow and shine and radiate fun, your teeth are
glowing in the sun.

My teenage girl, you hide your smile behind a
hand, apparently a trend in tik tok land.

But your smile is enchanting, your smile is
sweet and as your mother, I love to see your
teeth.

The happiness facilitator

Feed them, clothe them, keep them warm,
protect them from all of life storms.

Sound familiar? Is this you?

You've got the job, now do it well in all you do.

Jessica Joy

Born in my heart,
I loved you from the very start,
Your chubby red cheeks, your eyes; chocolate
and half moon,
Being your mum couldn't happen too soon.

Jessica, my high energy, sunshine source,
You have taught me more than I could learn on
any course.

I'm incredibly proud of all you do,
My chocolate eyed little boo.

Ruby Blossom

Being your mum is never boring, together we
have faced each challenging soaring.

Ruby you're brave, unique and bold and I can't
wait for your story to unfold,

You my daughter are made to do great things,
you're resilient, determined and strong, you'll
never sing anyone else's song.

Never change my baby girl, your chapters are
yet to unfurl.

I'll always be standing from the side, cheering
you along, together we are strong.

Just do your best

If everyday you wake up and you do your best,
each night on your pillow, your head can rest.

But do not forget, having a rest is also doing
your best.

Adhd magic

Let me take you if I may into the world of
ADHD magic,

The high energy is second to none, in one day
the ADHD brain can get a weeks work done.

The talking, the story telling, the detail, the fun,
just be prepared to listen, the adhd brain will talk
for hours at it's own admission.

The loyalty, the bonds, the sociability and the
intense feeling of each emotion, make the adhd
brain a truly good friend.

Then comes the focus, the determination, the
goals, matched with the energy a dream can be
sold.

But then comes the overwhelm, the distraction,
the stress, which can leave the ADHD brain in a
real mess.

Adhd is not a 'naughty kid', it's a brain that's
different and unique, ADHD is a super power
not afraid to speak.

Curves for days

This body of mine has let me down, on four
occasions it's completely shut down,

It's left me in really severe pain and of every
emotion it would drain.

On days and weeks I couldn't leave my bed,
'order the mobility scooter' the consultant said.

But on all of the other days this body has served
me well, it's allowed me to dance, to walk, to
stretch and bend, this is miraculous when you
felt like your darkness would never end.

So in a world where bodies are shamed,
celebrate your curves, I will exclaim.

Because all bodies are good bodies and yours is
too, every curve, every wobble is part of you.

Life is far too short to question your size, like a
curvy queen you just need to rise.

Friends

I have a group of group of friends, they're called the flamingo flock,

Not a pigeon between us, in unity we all rock.

One common purpose and that is to have fun,
Being with the flamingos always brings out the sun.

We dance, we drink, we laugh, we cheer, our embrace of the 4th decade is crystal clear.

We put the G into glamour, whilst dancing in converse boots and next time we are dancing we'll be wearing sequin suits.

So when you find your gorgeous tribe, hold them close and near, for these women are all shamazing and are the pure flamingo vibe.

The teenage sleep over

Hello My G, how are you?

Big Chezza in the house, how do you do?

The formula is simple, have a chat, make pizza,
expect 15 minutes of time, then the teenagers
disappear.

They'll arrive back when they're hungry and
make wake up time clear.

Do not wake the teenagers, it's a scary,
dangerous sight. Only one for the brave or
stupid, be prepared to take full flight.

The next weekend it starts all again…

Hello My G, how are you?

Big Chezza in the house, how do you do?

Moving the mountain

Do the research, wear the suit, be articulate, give
softness the boot, make a threat, state your
worth, drop a name, be assertive with no shame.

Move the mountain.

On repeat, get set go, be relentless and let your
love show.

Keep going and never stop, your children are
worth your energy, every single drop.

Move the mountain, one little push at a time, be
relentless and let your love show.

When your voice shakes, do not stop.

Life is not about the gentle conversations, the chat about the weather, the compliments, the pleasantries and the passing of the time.

Life is about the conversations that make your voice shake, that make you hot under the collar, that feel frightful not delightful but are vital all the same.

Vital all the same as these conversations open thoughts, minds and hearts. When your voice shakes the conversation truly starts.

It took a footballer

I was a footballer,

Let us never forget,

The tories were happy for the children of the UK to go unfed.

I saw those families, I heard their tummies rumble.

Never trust a Tory, we've got you rumbled.

Thank goodness for that!

25

21 poems in 21 days,

I thought it was achievable,

I've written 15 in a day if they're rubbish, that's believable.

In summary, be happy, be strong, celebrate your curves and always get your virtual lipstick on!